# Bonetown

*Poems by*

STEVE EVANS



Wakefield Press

Wakefield Press
Box 2266
Kent Town
South Australia 5071

First published 1994



Edited by Graham Rowlands
Cover and book designed by Kerry Argent
Typeset by Clinton Ellicott
Printed and bound by Hyde Park Press, Adelaide

Cataloguing in publication data
Evans, Steve, 1952– .
Bonetown.
ISBN 1 86254 332 1.
I. Title.

A821.3

Promotion of this book has been assisted by the South Australian Government through the Department for the Arts and Cultural Development.

Publication of this book was assisted by the Commonwealth Government through the Australia Council, its arts funding and advisory body.

# Contents

..........

**Bonetown**
The Quiet 3
Tin 4
Baths 8
Heatwave 10
Galahs 12
Our Plymouth of the Lake 13
Jetty 16
Fishing 17
Squid 18
Dabbing 19
Harry 20
Preserves 22
School House 24
Kites 25
Tar 26
Phosphorus 27
Water Tanks 28
A Country Dance 29
Old Dump 30
In the Pink 31
After Work 32

Hands 33
Naked 34
Flux 36
Old Codgers 39
Bones 41

**Snakes and Angels**
Numbers 45
Lightning 48
The Jesuses 50
The Periodic Table 52
Kimono 54
The King is Dead 56
Electric 57
Ice Man 58
Paranoia 59
Snake 60
Dreams 63
Flies 64
Crows 65
Knife and Fork 66
Ideograms 67
Language 69
Moon 71
The Observer's Guide to Angels 73
On the Tenth Planet 74

**Satellites**


| | |
|---|---|
| Going Home | 79 |
| Thomsons | 81 |
| Hotels | 84 |
| Divorce | 86 |
| Flying | 87 |
| Together | 88 |
| Saints | 89 |
| Finger Painting | 91 |
| Children | 92 |
| The Fruit Quiz | 93 |
| Skin and Bone | 94 |
| Maybe | 96 |
| Contentment | 98 |
| Rendezvous | 99 |

**Author's note**

Poems in this collection have appeared in *The Canberra Times*, *The Fremantle Arts Review*, *Island*, *Kangaroo*, *Larrikin*, *Luna*, *Mattoid*, *Opinion*, *Oz Arts*, *Prints*, *Quadrant*, *Scarp*, *Southern Review*, *Southland*, *The Sydney Morning Herald*, *Verso*, and *Voices*, and the anthologies, *Friendly Street Reader Nos. 8, 14, 17 and 18.* Some have also been broadcast on *Radio 5UV* and *ABC Radio*.

Thanks are due to Jeri Kroll, Jan Owen and Barry Westburg for their insights and willing encouragement, and also to David Gilbey, James Bradley and Graham Rowlands for their helpful comments on these poems.

Some poems were completed with the assistance of a grant from the South Australian Department for the Arts and Cultural Heritage.

# Bonetown

## The Quiet

a train on the other side of town
might be the only
moving thing in the world
you hear each jarrah sleeper groan
each turned wheel sing
its scissoring

a truck horn goose-calls in fog
someone else awake
later from a distant ridge
a dog barks at its echo

the bedside clock
says it's hours till the sun
so many left to listen to sounds
clear as those over water
your town in its lake of sleep

## Tin

1. a rain tank
in retirement
becomes home for
ducks or dogs
when water's found
the weaknesses
and gone
leaving only a
cylinder of echoes
to be tipped and rolled
booming
to its new place
under the pepper tree

houses also built of tin
imported panels of
delicately patterned ceilings
or (in the cheaper part of town)
walls of beaten sheets still
advertising Best Blue Flame
Petroleum

2. all the other notes
metal plays on the senses

first in the flecks
of galvanised fences
alight in afternoon sun
xylophones for kids with sticks

then under the waves of
a lifted sheet of iron
the yellow rectangle of grass
and a woken snake unwinding

fingers dipped
in rings of metal
permanently porpoising
through hoops of gold

mercury's droplet mirrors
circling in the dish
of my palm

the suddenly whipping strands
of loosened wire that separate
three fingers from a hand

a camp-fire billy swung
in the clearing
by a moon-drenched creek

tin ducks in a side-show
peppered with shot
paddling back for more

a saved ball of
brain-wrinkly foil
the stuff that shivers fillings

the strange can
at the back of the shelf
unlabelled

the first faint drum-roll
hail on a tin roof
showing off

soldering gone haywire
tinning useless
silvery pools

3. such jewellery
these treasures
and each metal's cut
heals differently
the scars as varied
as signatures
this by corrugated iron
that by stainless steel

you hold the hard edge
of the world

**Baths**

old bathtubs in their slow migration
move instinctively from house to field
from lather and steam
to cold contemplation
claw-feet deep in grass
their flat mimicry of skies
occasionally troubled
by thirsty horses

on a day exhausted by heat
this tub in the shade of eucalypts
cornered by barbed wire's
spiky knots
is as round as a 1950 Buick
voluptuous as a Rubens nude
and too cool to resist
I strip and sink
a cloud of debris like plankton
stews around me

just me?
in my sprawling contentment
I picture them
all over the countryside
a run-aground fleet of cast-iron dinghies
reclaiming its former owners
the land suddenly peppered
with their naked figures
bolt upright and soaking wet
almost as startled as the livestock
gathered there to drink

## Heatwave

day one –
cantankerous kids
the hose soft as licorice
a sudden richness of spiders
and persistent flies
I snatch sun-hardened clothes
from the line
dance scalding dirt
back to the house
ice-cubes clatter in the sink

day two –
damp towels hung on screen doors
the strategically timed opening
and closing of windows
fanning beds' limp bodies
wet hankies at foreheads and necks
while the stupid distant music
of a council sprinkler
flickers over the slick clay
of the town square
on day two
no one is talking
to anyone else

day three –
sleep is impossible
I stand on the cement floor
of the bathroom
see my mother hosing
a shimmer of insects
in the dark garden
and sink my face
in a basin of clear
cold water

I'm never coming up

## Galahs

pretty as prunus blossom
scattered in the distant air
until I hear them
coming to gate-crash
the orchard again

in their confused party attire
spiky punk crests
and outfits kitsch as coconut-ice
grey cardigans over lurid pink
they're a curious mix of grandmother
and larrikin
(The Sex Pistols
out of Barbara Cartland)

wheeling in loud circles
above our ragged trees
vivid anti-Buddhas
screeching Strine

## Our Plymouth of the Lake

1. he drives into the lake
sits wondering how he's done it
with water past his ankles
and climbing
his hands still upon the wheel

the lake under a half moon
next swallows his knees
he lets out the clutch pedal
and relaxes his grip on the wheel
he would consult the owner's handbook
but suspects this situation
is not mentioned

the lake sighs to his waist
the headlights fade
and he wonders how much deeper

perhaps he would start the car again
and turn it with the flow
but there is no flow
this is a lake, not a river
a destination, not a trip
he sits in a twilight world
as if floating in and out of sleep
half-woken

on the far shore
a scattering of small lights
one his home
he inspects the few stars
the moon on the bonnet
ponders the guaranteed grip
of his new All-Weather tyres
now deep in mud
hears the clicking
of the engine's contractions
thinks that this spot
is roughly where
he came off last time

he considers how
you hear of people
parking their car after an accident
never driving again
stories of forty-year-old Dodges
discovered in the dust
of long-locked sheds

it's give up driving
or give up drinking
he thinks
so he locks the doors
and swims for home

2. the tyres' twin ruts
through the grass
soon disappeared
since then
the whirr of insects
the lap and lull of
water against the car
it remained
predictable
a watermark
off the dirt road
mud, rust and algae
the just visible roof we passed every day
and jumped off in summer
with all the other kids

perfect as a stone
in a Japanese temple garden
our Plymouth of the Lake

## Jetty

a wooden centipede
painted with squid juice
the gaps between timbers jammed
with broken cockle shells
jagged remnants of angels' wings

the grain-ship harnessed to its side
is scuffed where the jetty first
rebuffed its advances
rust and scratches in a patched
crust of red primer and raw metal
Jackson Pollock marine

a jarrah forest cut and squared
a platform which fishermen patrol
their gear carried in trolleys
made from old prams or lawnmowers
the Victa heading out
as if to mow the sea

## Fishing

my father removes a fish hook
from my finger
with a worn bait knife
a little hole made bigger
but so delicately
I can't believe he is cutting me
the blood falling in small
red stars on the dull silver
of three caught salmon
at our feet

I wash my hand in a bucket
of sea water
and hope for a scar
the water below us
performing reckless
miracles of light

## Squid

a graceful underwater kite
hoist from its clear peculiar sky
into another thinner one
a mottled flap of
mud-coloured indignation
slapped onto the jetty

fool for the simplest
imitation of fish
it squirms by a red plastic bucket
flusters through its wardrobe
first slick mother-of-pearl
then ghostly
white-as-English flesh

a gout of ink
scribbled on the tarred wood
spills a signature of useless defiance

## Dabbing

I walk a halo through
the shallows of a summer night
a bucket in a tethered tube
nudging me gently as a dog

in the hazy lit disk under my lamp
the beak of a garfish appears
its body a Dada knife-handle
drowsing into reach, already mine

I scoop it like a dreaming child
so softly it hardly knows it's caught
and another, another, twenty-four
come swooning to my hand

in the bucket a complete set
of sleek hypnotised cutlery
silvery opal
shaped like fish

## Harry

with a moving extra skin
that hugged and moved
and sang to him
Harry rode his bicycle through town
collecting empties

a Las Vegas showman
in his suit of lights
had nothing on Harry
whose best and only suit
was made of bees

Harry the Human Hive
dressed in thousands of tiny
living pelts
Harry the Queen Bee
smiling inside his swarming skin

I waited on the gate
to watch a humming arm
scoop bottles
from the footpath
Harry on parade

in a shack of sloping iron
a wood-stove and spring bed
his savings stacked outside in a glassy bank
that filtered sunlight green and blue
Harry poured honey into jars

there were rumours
Harry in the city once a year
spending big
a sweet week of women and liquor
not a bee in sight

but I knew where he belonged
even when his collecting ceased
Bottle-O Harry
Queen Bee Harry
Harry the Human Hive

honey drunk
the drowned bees
left a tiny slick
on the surface
of the creek by his shack

the others found the
body in the wood
made themselves at home
and honeycomb'd
his skull

## Preserves

always the sugary froth of jam
simmering at the lip
of a vast metal pot
and glassy cylinders in rows
that catch the light
there's nothing that won't fit
in a jar

the rich and juicy
almost foreign language
of the inventory she reels off
quinces, peaches, apricots
locquats, cumquats, plums and pears

her catchment extended from
her own back yard
to the neighbourhood, the town
days she spent travelling
for that perfect crop
rumoured in a nearby state

the bartering and the ribbons
the pantry bigger than the house
baskets of stone fruits
barrows of marrows
and midnight sessions
selecting the best
the unblemished God's own
that will glisten
seductive as a starlet's pout
when the judges approach

the world's preserved here
in a jar
the moment stopped
no more than Nature would have done
had it the time
and her skill

## School House

the walls are weatherboard
stark surfaces of smooth enamel
too hot to touch
overlapped like closed venetian blinds

they suddenly open
the school house blinks
becomes an almost Japanese house
delicate as a paper fan

unattached
the floating roof sails away
trailing the clattering planks
of the walls like the flailing
tail of a kite

## Kites

brown paper and glue
a skeleton of umbrella spokes
spread on the kitchen table
like a deconstruction kit
a maze of pick-up-sticks

the paddock launching
of a scrawny diamond
five nose-dives into dirt
then something hauling at my hands
through the spool of string
wanting that rickety contraption
much more than I

weeks later
the wreckage seen
broken on a telephone wire
miles from home
is just like mine
but so are the next two
on that long aerial graveyard

## Tar

he propped his shovel against
the flat-top truck
parked his heeler at the door
and came in from the road-gang
crossing the lino of the grocery floor
to buy three pounds of butter
a black gummy track to the counter
and back

opened the packets right outside
took up fat handfuls of yellow
and rubbed himself clean of tar
like a strange holy man
in navy singlet and stained hat
glistening on the footpath
in our town
as his dog licked at the ground

**Phosphorus**

the Murphy boys were
constant experimenters
slaves to chemical mysteries
mixing exotic cocktails of kerosene
and other unattended treasures from
garden shed or chemistry lab
both the perfect hosts
offering first sips to inquisitive guests
lighting wicks to explosive potions
and daring each other not to run

but Brian was weird
even for a Murphy
Brian I remember
in a chemistry lesson
holding raw phosphorus
while a hole burnt in his palm
a look of queer pleasure
on his face
something he knew
and could not share

## Water Tanks

behind our house
the introverted mass of the tank
was a snare-drum constantly brushed
by a pepper tree
a muted gong to the knuckles' enquiry
up and down the scale of its rings

fetching for the kettle or washing-up
the rinsing of a sister's soapy hair
meant drawing from that cold, tideless dam
time to wait and dream
while the water rattled enamel
gravity let loose in jugs and sloshing pots
swivelling basins and bell-heavy bowls

years later for a prank
Tim Webster dropped into a school-yard tank
as if through a hole in the ice
and didn't come up at all

this curious column
a pillar to lean on
and think before pouring a cupful
of wrigglers to drink
its elephant sides climbed
to discover always in that private dark
a saucer of light afloat
a face looking up that might be mine
or his

## A Country Dance

the welcoming committee
is the Northern Areas Boxing Champion
waiting between dances
waiting behind the outside toilets
to rearrange your face with a bottle
your teeth with a brick

he'll think of some excuse
you may have danced with his
could-have-been
you may have looked his way
but mostly you're new in town

against a gentle chorus of
gossip from the Ladies
and the pale light from
the window of the Town Hall
he'll introduce himself
tell his story on your face
blow by blow
a job at the factory
a language in his fists
more persuasive than words
welcome welcome welcome

## Old Dump

on this older side of town
anywhere I scuff the ground
turns up metal
strange treasure in spots not
marked with an X

the earth saw-toothed
weed-wild
a living thing
all spines and stings

inches below my feet
bits of tin and twisted rust
barbed wire itching to get out
like shrapnel in the body
old thorns below the skin
the truth coming home

**In the Pink**

near the pellet works
the fall-out of ore dust
leaves everything
footpaths, walls and roofs
the soft pink of face powder
old girl's make-up
a permanent sunset rose

I run my finger through it
on a window ledge
and wonder what the cure is
for sunset in the lungs

## After Work

at the knock-off whistle
packs of bikes
left the factory gate
not greyhound thin or urgent
as today's fluorescent pretenders
the BSAs and Raleighs in sombre green
took their time
splitting at this corner or that
slow pedalled
spreading through the town

some paused a while
propped in rows against the pub
the pitted chrome circles
of springs
under leather saddles
and their curved bars
antlers interlocked

later leaving
in leisurely ones and twos
homing through the small streets
the pampered ones to laundries
leant against washing-machines
or into sheds
the others to side fences
a long night under a powder of stars
gathering frost

## Hands

past the church-and-pub-and-two-house towns
past the shy dirt-road towns
are all the little Edens
farms named in hopeless spots
for dreams of plenty
sheds gone diagonal over the years
a back paddock
where oil-dark hands
work on a reluctant Nuffield

hands
playing the dull music
of spanners against a tool box

hands shaping the alphabet
in childish letters
not quite begging the bank to wait

hands running grit across the slopes
of a midnight wife

hands pouring a pocketful
of bullets when the market's down

hands at a late tea
folding into each other
for grace

## Naked

a puddle of clothes
on a Bonetown corner one night
(plaid shirt, blue singlet
worn overalls and boots
even the undies and socks)
someone swallowed by a UFO
drawn naked into dazzling air
shrinking from all earthly connections
no use for King Gees where he went

or perhaps
he saw the burning bush
and detoured around the rest of his life
either way
one more not coming home
evaporated between the pub
and his small front gate

more likely on a summer's night
three blocks from The Drover's Arms
and five drinking hours from work
the missing man suddenly saw
the sense of nudity
or the senselessness of clothes
and strode home free

staring at the modest heap
a puzzle under a stuttering street light
I felt the skin beneath
my shirt begin to itch

## Flux

1. I stop my bike
on the summer outskirts
of a country childhood
far from shade and houses
the air combustible
the shirt tied at my neck
clinging to a film of sweat

ahead
the snake basks
on heat-hazed bitumen
a dark vein flickering
on the grey skin of the road

I hurl my fear
into urgent parabolas of stone
until the snake stirs
slips into a dry paddock
as if the earth tipped
poured it away

2. others through the years
a quick bump
under the tyres of the family car
or a movement glimpsed
in the shadow of the hen-house
a few nearly trodden on
then engaged in that curious dance
where the snake always leads

the luckless ones
red-eyed and brilliant
sliced into twitching segments
watched superstitiously
till sunset

3. now, after so long
a meeting at midnight
on my own ground

the refrigerator's pool of light
spills across my bare legs
and the floor repeats its whispering
a brown scarf of flesh
winds past my feet
a fluid trespass
towards the door

in the morning
a turned-out belt of skin
at the doorstep
I fold it over my arm
the yellow grass
sways beyond the meagre
rectangle of lawn

## Old Codgers

will travel the length of a jetty
unbidden
to show you the right way
to bait a hook
while their other hand's
fat sausage fingers
wind tasselled makings
into a fag

they remember Menzies
as that young bloke
and the war, well
ya wouldn't think we won it
to look around ya
and kids these days
wouldn't know hard work
if it fell on 'em
don't know how good they've got it
ah, but things have changed
ya can't get a decent beer no more
it's all these chemicals
hey, I think you've got one
no?
give us it here
no, he's gone

and so it goes
a potted history of the favoured
footy team
a few tips for the survival
of Australian culture
long stare over the choppy waves
to the thin line of failing light
on the horizon

they managed all those years
without metrics
know the true measures
are still 'some' and 'a few'
not kilos and litres
they ask for two bob o' chips
and check their change
for real money
they're such easy targets
and you'll always miss

## Bones

sneaking outside at midnight
to stand in the bottom acre
where boney-arsed cows
a clutch of kit-bags in conference
lie snuffling their misty flags
into winter air

above us
dumb creatures all
the clear sky's wrack of stars
the bones of space
like these rough sticks
we're hung upon
brief definitions
of place in the world

I turn back through wet grass
to the abandoned house
navigating by the small square
of my old bedroom window
still familiar across the dark
where my father stood
twenty years ago
watching me out here
thinking himself unseen

# Snakes and Angels

## Numbers

### *Home Truths*

most people think them common as stones
plain as air
but here are some home truths about
numbers

for a start
fractions don't grow into whole numbers
that's gypsy talk
and favourite numbers are unreliable
no allegiance beyond their latest whim
they'll use you

you think numbers can be house-broken
trained as pets
numbers play along
only do tricks when it suits them
that wildness remains
even in the Highest Prime

we all know integers
closed and secretive
pompous as pedigreed Pekes
and Pi is just tedious
an endless freight train of digits
rattling to a self-glorious tune

*My Experience*
I had a small number once
it was almond-shaped and quiet
until it bit the dog
so I swapped it for a black biro
the number came back
and the dog ran away
I didn't return the pen

*My Sister's Experience*
my sister went out with one
and was never seen again

*Their Origin and Some Other Matters*
on their origin there is just confusion
some prefer the Arabian theory
some the Chinese
there is also the binary sect
others say comets seeded them
into our atmosphere

metrication just shuffled them
they saw through that

once the Prime Numbers were king
now they are outcast
exiled freaks and hoboes
it's a long story

*Numbers' Humour*
they only have one joke
they believe they're numerically superior

*Final Advice on Numbers*
there is no safety in numbers
they get in where you least expect
they are survivors
the cockroaches of abstraction
never trust a number
they are not like us
the only good number
is an imaginary one

## Lightning

remind yourself
the bark of thunder
this pocket of stillness and glowing air
as you walk home is only show
but caught in the open
a vague luminescence attaching to everything
like faint haloes
you feel vulnerable
recalling whole cricket teams clean-bowled
by such a heavenly dance and racket

tell yourself
it's not a question of punishment
nothing so personal
just an equation to be completed
through whatever's convenient
be practical
would being in a crowd
reduce the odds?
an amulet?
a hat?

if it helps
the instructions are these
    don't linger by tall objects
    or metal ones
    don't dawdle
    present a small target
    crouch
    run if you like
    most of all
    pray it finds you resistible
on the other hand
you could stand straight
hoping it will detour
in deference to courage
but if it even thinks of you
if your hair should suddenly prickle
would a car accident have been better?

it's close
a momentary flicker and growl
in the next suburb
too close
but who knows
if it happens
that instant of belonging
to both earth and sky
somewhere there may be a cult
that will think you blessed

## The Jesuses

six strange Jesuses
at my door
one's fat
one's bald
and one sells brushes
another's just plain bored
one winks
one peddles life insurance
they all give out a yawn
one wears trousers
one a dress
one is French
and one Chinese
one hawks religious relics
one sells his autograph
one wears knee-high cowboy boots
one a curled moustache
five of them sing in unison
the other forgets the song
one shows me his appendix scar
one takes my photograph
three of them want to bless me
three want to buy my car
one's fiddling with his halo
one throws up on the marigolds

a sudden embarrassed silence
they all consult their notebooks
then the tallest murmurs softly
'Sorry, wrong address!'
and they turn away

at the kerb
their mother waiting
angry in her car

**The Periodic Table**
*(from the Casper Lectures)*

we know these days
that the first elements
of the true periodic table
are Sunlight, Anxiety, Cardboard
and the colour Blue

current theory also hints at
a particle somewhere between
Cardboard and Blue
the original tape of Heartbreak Hotel
is a perfect fit
but this is so far pure conjecture
I prefer to wait for the evidence

the next four elements are, of course
the Scottish Accent, the Coefficient of
Friction Between Lovers' Skin
the Scent of Eucalyptus
and Mexico City, 1903

dogs by the way
have an even simpler table
consisting of bits of string
and something on the bottom of your shoe
but can we afford to feel smug
who once got the planets so wrong?

remember how early man used to think
there were only six elements in all
mostly related to brown paper bags
and lint found in trouser cuffs?
how we thought there were other signs
of the zodiac besides Gecko?

the other nineteen elements
I'll address another time
(their electron steps are Astairean
and their orbits increasingly strange)
but now let's talk about the shortest lived
yet most common one
Sex

**Kimono**

a gift for her he said
the kimono he'd brought
drifted wide across the bed
sailed down in a spell of lights
silk shot through with little fires
and as it lay it seemed to her
an aerial glimpse of a land she knew
but couldn't name

in the upper right of its dark map
a gully wind shook small pink
buds of eucalypts
under a clouded moon
and on the shoulder
streets familiar as a dream
formed in miniature
but when she looked closer
shivered and dissolved

drawing nearer to the waist
she saw a young girl crouching
a rocket in a milk bottle
blue paper waiting for a match
and a shower of silver tears
a clattering flower of sparks

before this too went
she saw on the thin
hand which held the match
her mother's ring glittering
in the small flame
like water beaded on the bottle's rim

she jerked back from this impossibility
and it was only cloth there in her room
intricate work but merely thread
even careless on the hem
ragged and confused where
in the light of a small window
a tiny couple stood
a man sailing a kimono
into the air above a bed
and a woman
happy
who was not her

## The King is Dead

the paper says
the King of the Gypsies is dead
I spread it over the hotel bed
to read

the King is dead
it says
and no one will wash or comb their hair
for the three days he'll sit
in his small caravan
in a European backwater
circled by candles and flowers
propped in his best suit
waiting for a successor

I am three days in this small town
in this small room
without candles or flowers
we are waiting both
but the King of the Gypsies is dead

## Electric

she shook her hands of water
after dishes at the sink
two rosellas crossed the window
their Joseph coats afire
and with her eyes still on them
she leant to flick the kettle on

a chink that day
an unexpected opening
through which she put her hand
reached in to the x-ray land
of cartoon victims stuck in sockets
or primitive translucent fish
plugged in to that same circuitry

her body in unexpected bloom
blue aura'd in the kitchen
shivering in a private pool of light
and all the switches
in the house's net of wires
suddenly opened to her as she danced
everything finally possible

## Ice Man

Latin came and went
the Industrial Revolution
not even a whisper in
the back of his mind
the symphonion turning overhead
played the small white
holes of its static
that unheard music his lullaby
while he slept and waited
this leather thing
that was a man
the body in the freezer
on slow de-frost
straw in his shoes
and a glacier for a tomb
what pharaoh wouldn't have envied him?

in peat-bogs, ash-beds and gravel-pits
the ones and twos by ritual or accident
the hundreds in whole villages
laid down to muddy sleep
and later this afternoon
on an Austrian alp
his two newest apprentices
in fluorescent lime and pink
will begin their own slow journey
swaddled in avalanche

## Paranoia

life's a thriller
where everyone's a spy
everyone a double agent
for another double agent
and you trust yourself
least of all

## Snake

who needs fingers?
all those bony hooks
encumbrances
I'm the simplicity of
an exclamation mark
all hip and hipless
I could be your belt
your skipping rope
the long rope of fear itself
flickering at your ankles

some of us subtle as clerks
in anonymous greys and browns
others brilliant as our cousins
the birds of paradise
diamond backs
vermilion and hypnotic blue
colours loud as the Moulin Rouge
but twice as beautiful
all licking air
for the scent of you

the temptation of Eve?
she convinced me!
I was the very sinew of Paradise
now Eden's just a joke
bad P.R.
'they shall take up serpents'
says the Book of Mark
the fools of The Church of
The Lord Jesus Christ believe it
their hands full of our whispering plaits
one day we'll strike
them all down
now just one or two for fun

I'm a tongue-kissing
tongue-twisting core-sample
of places you'll never see
a low-life smooth beguiler
in some lands a delicacy
as we say
one man's mate
is another man's python

sidewinding
I leave the hollow other me
an empty sleeve behind
my ghost
a discarded wrapper
brittle stocking

I'm my own slow dance
soft as babies' lips
a slinky rhythm master
cutlery-tongued and tunnel-shaped
a tube of muscle
with my eye on you

## Dreams

*all birds and mammals dream*
*except the spiny ant-eater*
Newsweek

sudden musical ability welling like tears
instant nakedness in a public place
a kiss from a beautiful stranger
falling
just as there are only three kinds of joke
there are only two of dream
those of hopes
those of fears

we all twitch like dog paws
in sleepy ecstasy or fright
except one
better than mystics
the spiny ant-eater clears its mind
of even the shadow of an ant
but there are other creatures
more mysterious than the dreamless

when fish dream
they dream they are fish
when snakes dream
they dream they are snakes
and when lawyers dream
they dream they are lawyers

this makes them dangerous

## Flies

the first aerobics instructors
inventors of the great
Australian salute
primitive as rocks
flies are rudimentary
micro-dinosaurs
single-minded as wind-up toys

some cranky black and stupid
some regal beetle-blue
untreasured gaudies
head-butting useless Morse
at every window
plunging mouth-divers
joy-riding your inward breath
living on instinct
ear, nose and
throat specialists

bend close
you'll hear the buzz
and hum
they're always singing
the fly anthem –
got no honey
just got shit
nectar sweeter
but not so much of it

## Crows

those wise-cracking
black scraps of wind
dizzily swoop and swoon
down a blustering sky
clowns inside their dark trappings
their rasping bark admonition
and clever remark
they dwindle
fullstops on the horizon
laughing the distance in
at their own wit and cunning

it's a comedy
solemn as undertakers
for these unlit darknesses
sombre as
crows

## Knife and Fork

mashed potato's plough
honey-slickers and pea flickers
impromptu drumsticks

a service in silvered rows
however elegant
on its velvet bed
is still just tooth and claw
cut and clutch
chopsticks with pretensions
they mimic us

it's primitive
this stab and grab
that makes the world
digestible

## Ideograms

the strangest common word in English
as long as Maori place names
but less pronounceable
is a story in twenty six staccato parts
the cryptic remnants show
an arrowhead and something like
  a crude knuckle duster
    followed by a hoof-print
      and the handle of a cup
a broken comb
  a tattered flag
    but what's the significance
      of the carpenter's clamp
beside a damaged bed-frame
  or the ingot
    and the hook dreaming of fish?
      it continues, more obscure
a hat-rack (perhaps) but no hat
  and a dog-leg
    by a paper crown
      a kind of gate
a fish mouth clearly
  the handle of a sword
    the symbol for sperm and egg
      then an abbreviated slippery dip

with a snake at its base
    (there's always a snake)
        an unreadable road sign
            and the cup the handle forgot
cleavage next
    (so sex comes into it again)
        and arms upflung in alarm
            or celebration
then an unknown quantity
    (the signature of millions)
        a question in a wine glass
            and lastly a slash of lightning

mysterious as Beowulf
this noisy song that children learn by heart
an odd caterpillar of capital shapes
printed in frieze
above the blackboards of thousands
of primary school class rooms
the alphabet

## Language

*learning a language*
*left behind when the ice melted*
Penelope Shuttle

mathematical symbols and formulae
a chalky whirlwind of ideas
the rough families of glyphs and runes
stabbed into rock
pictographs and thorny ideograms
scratched in clay
graceful brush-licked cursives
and moody cyrillics carved with crayon
their meanings smudge my fingers

shy acronyms too
jargon and other condensations
the introverted and inbred
dialectic and specialist
tribal and sectarian
reaching out
but not too far

the physical
accents pronounced with fists
and slashed seats
coins dragged through the red duco
of a new Mercedes
secret handshakes
the sneer and spit
the beating out of fear
the uniforms
especially those unknown
to the wearers
all the practised curlicues
and embellishments
of signatures
the long dance of self

they say every tongue can be learnt
that each has a Rosetta Stone buried somewhere
and even the weather
this planet's monologue
with its many willing interpreters
not quite getting it right
will yield one day
but they're wrong
one language refuses translation
there's no code to break
the silence between you and me

**Moon**

the faintest light draws me to a doorway
and there you are again
unreachable ghostly fruit
on a branch of cloud
I'm over the moon about you
in all your costumes
and you're always over me

I loved you as
the blue moon of Kentucky
the monsoonal blood moon too
the old ivory of
your yellow harvest moon
all the standards
but you, old china
my old chipped plate
you turn the blind eye
a white hole floating in space
to all this

well I've seen the cow jumping over
the man in you
and I don't care

my scarred pearl
king of tides
of salt, blood and madness
I'll still carry your
beams home in a jar
I'll hum your music
summoning howls and fits
while there's still that silver shilling
a searchlight through the window
keeping me from sleep

## The Observer's Guide to Angels

*angels without portfolio*
Miroslav Holub

it's the little things you notice
they wear ordinary clothes
but hum next year's hit song
sometimes forget about gravity
stepping too lightly off the kerb
they may have difficulty with
the concept of money
giving the shopkeeper change
or speak a language you've
never heard but somehow understand

angels can't drive
or remember jokes
they have trouble with shoelaces
and instructions on the backs of packets
they may compliment you
on your shoulder blades

some gone feral are sleeping rough
and hanging out on street corners
talking tough
helpless as dumped kittens
they kiss like Brigitte Bardot
and follow you home
but you can't keep them
not even the fallen ones

## On the Tenth Planet

on the tenth planet
every citizen can choose any
one of his neighbours' possessions

on the tenth planet
rap music is an offence punishable
with six hours of cabaret

on the tenth planet
dolphins are a pest
known to carry off the young

on the tenth planet
drink-driving is the approved
form of population control

on the tenth planet
everyone is named Bob
(it's all in the pronunciation)

on the tenth planet
possession of a piano accordion
is only permitted with a doctor's certificate

on the tenth planet
all politicians are required
to go naked

on the tenth planet
everyone loses their
wings at puberty

on the tenth planet
accountancy is illegal
but practised in secret by rebels

on the tenth planet
they laugh at the notion of
life on Uth

# Satellites

## Going Home

they haunt me
here in a narrow street
their favourite tune spilling
unexpectedly from an upstairs window
even the colours in the park
imitate their garden in Australia
at least the sky is less intense
grey and oddly luminous
it is reassuringly foreign

on my first visit
stepping into this strange country
source of my parents' story
is to understand the many
inflections of childhood
the subtle insinuations
of polished wooden floors
and the careful placing
of a vase of flowers
certain music in
the back of my mind
I'd thought forgotten

they left here forty years ago
and have not returned
but these smells and sounds
were somehow waiting in me
and in each street and shop
the ghosts with his voice
and her eyes
welcome me home

**Thomsons**

1. they like to yell
an argument's a tonic
invitation to slamming doors
and weeping declarations

they clomp the earth
asserting their presence
their right to
clomp the earth

they love noise
a bath of energy
the volume knob
always on 10

2. loudest of all the men
who go to sea young
send postcards from exotic
ports and make
brief occasional returns
adjusting with difficulty
to the shore
mouths brimming with commands
scared to stay for long

first words they never heard
seasons and childhoods missed
marriages measured by
their long absences
and gaps in family albums
kids tucked into Sunday best
taking trips with mother
to visit other Thomson women

3. they're impulsive purchasers
of massive obstinate dogs
of indeterminate breed
and poor behaviour

proud if naive owners
of unusual cars
Jowett Javelins and Borgward Isabellas
in which the children are
embarrassed to be seen
sinking low in the back seat

4. a warring tribe
quick-tempered and teasers when young
still short-fused when grown
their own sharpest critics
they are their own people
loyal to the Thomsons
they love to hate

5. Thomsons –
looking at my son
I see half of one
and realise
it's the other half
I worry about

## Hotels

arriving late
you're steered to a room
alive still with the smell of urine
and cigarettes

the shower's a drizzle
and the towel abrasive as steel wool
on the bedside table there's
an ashtray stolen from another hotel
an electric jug and tea-bag
but no cup
the TV bolted to the wall
has one fuzzy channel
the bed's a squeaking valley
the three tissues in the dispenser
will be counted in the morning

bored, you read the Bible
at least there's still a Bible
though someone has underlined passages
and torn out the Song of Solomon
the closest you were going to get
to sex or poetry

at five in the morning
another argument in the next room
above the noise of the plumbing
you lie back and watch the moon
white against a winter sky
same moon over a house you left
where light will soon
spill from a kitchen window
tea leaves cast a sodden arc
onto a rose bush
and a table cloth float down

another breakfast and early departure
back on the road
past the unopened shops
and into a flatness of paddocks
that will come to midday's
shimmering ambiguities
as if uncertain what shape to take

you will enter them freely
losing yourself
thinning to air

**Divorce**

is
half the usual clothing on the line
opening a dark house
an absence of furniture

is
paying more attention
to your appearance
so no one can say you've
let yourself go since the . . .
friends being too busy
or talking about
the weather instead of the . . .

is
getting someone else's mail
answering a phone
that should have rung
in another suburb
another planet

is
a towel with a stranger's monogram
a half-empty bed
if you won the bed
and
retrieving her photo
for a final look
again

**Flying**

distance entertains us
with its tricks
awash with air
the wrinkled earth shrinks away
a puddling of little lakes
stares at the sky
like briefly lit eyes
of animals at night
a slick thread of water
like unwinding cotton
wriggles down dark bush slopes
clouds imitate
the white heads of cauliflower

in sleepy semaphore
a bored hostess conducts
a safety routine we'll never need
up here there's no danger
no success or failure
just a narcotic suspension
we float harmless and unharmed
remote from sad arrivals
and anticlimax
so many of us
drunk on detachment
drifting
pretending destinations
flight junkies
with the new disease
Fear of Landing

## Together

she'd bring a bottle
I'd bring the glass
we went together that way

she'd bring the itch
I'd bring the lotion
we went together that way

she'd bring the reason
I'd bring the tears
we went together that way

she'd bring the accident
I'd bring the car
we went together that way

she'd bring the moonlight
I'd bring the sky
we went together that way

she'd bring the needle
I'd bring the vein
we went together that way

I'd bring the words
she'd bring the sense
we went together that way

but that's all over now
that's all over now

**Saints**

to Saint Casper
patron saint of those trying
to start an old mongrel car
thank you

to Saint Julio
who watches over those easily
confounded by household devices
can-openers
clothes driers
vacuum cleaners
my usual blessings

to Saint Felicity
guardian of birth control
have mercy upon me
again

to Saint Ira
protector of matching socks
Saint Whoever You Are
responsible for warding off
traffic jams
broken laces
burst zips
I've invoked you all

but I'm caught here
shaving at the morning mirror
where there is no grace
no resort
or fallback argument
and of the armies of saints
none dares help me

how easily we are
ruined by mirrors

## Finger Painting

the simplest things
first and only

in his world
we're stick figures
standing in severe landscapes
of would-be right-angles
and primary colours

reduced to our real selves

## Children

tangents and contradictions
they're half-measures
and too clever by half
innocent as snakes
and precociously Zen

koans and question marks
cunningly helpless lateral thinkers
brief morality plays with few morals

unboxed jacks-in-a-box
mirrors tossing back
our own buckled images

small beginnings
the slowest and least resistible coup

## The Fruit Quiz

our first fruit
from the baby tree
an unripe nectarine
fallen but found
and brought inside for show
is a bony ball

this from the woman who
years ago
placed a mango in my hand
try eating it she said
without once thinking
of sex –
I failed

I return the nectarine
a stone within a stone
to her palm
and wait for the question

## Skin and Bone

your silhouette a sinuous S
the dip and rise
of shoulder, waist and hip
almond oil lolls
warming in the cup of my hand
I'll be your geographer
mapping this wild terrain
with lips and fingertips
a chill of pleasure
xylophones my spine
considering what can be done
with skin and bone

the fingers' amazing articulation
each joint languidly
swivels in its pearly socket
the body's hinges
the angles and levers of love
I put my hands into a river
placing them on you
my molecules just fools
for your molecules

why coin superlatives?
better the soundless prayer
the whispers of flesh
and later the silent Z of your body
tucked against mine
you're my blue movie
my wild card
and we the scandal
the song of skin and bone

## Maybe

satellites speck the clear sky
but their spy-cameras
able to photograph a number plate
at thirty kilometres
are intent on other things
when we make love under stars
gymnastics in the lonely darkness
of the local park
or in our garden
sprawled between azaleas
and clumps of rhododendron
the smell of earth and you
small twigs and pieces of
grass clinging to your skin
an occasional inspection
by the neighbour's cat
and the light of an indifferent moon

carpet rash on elbows and knees
the occasional crash
of a favoured vase
colliding with wayward limbs
bones at play
everywhere
on the couch
on the floor
in the kitchen
out of doors
and (dare I dream)
one day maybe
in a bed

## Contentment

out there the wet road
spools around the hills
and a larrikin wagtail
flickers manically on my gate
as if strobe-lit

I turn from the window
from ribs of cloud
in a purpling sky
back to your eyes
Krishna blue

between a Monet dusk
and this rumpled bed
I've all the antics of Heaven
the contentment of ordinary miracles

**Rendezvous**

finally we dispense with conversation
leave the fireside
our drinks' wet rings on the table
for the cold upstairs

years ago we began
awkward as adolescents
undressing each other in a slow fever
eager and self-conscious
the senses shivered
and we gave ourselves up

tonight a country hotel
wind billows out of the fields
to buffet the window
and our music is rain's
soft nonsense

the charge is still there
your stockings gather in my fingers
your breathing shallows
nipples stiffen under my hands
in the half-light
older versions of those once stunned
to see themselves so bound
meet again the cool reassurance of skin

achieving this
what else can matter?
telling each other over and over
the one story
its ending always new

*Also by Steve Evans*

## Edison Doesn't Invent the Car
*and*
## Algebra

'By a process of lateral association and imaginative somersaults, the reader is transported (or seduced) into a quite bizarre or delightfully strange speculation. Evans combines humour, attentive observation and a conceptual intelligence that makes this poetry most satisfying, accessible, inventive.'

**David Gilbey**, *Southerly*

'Evans has a supple, playful vision. His approach is direct and his resource equal to almost anything that takes his attention.'

*Freemantle Arts Review*

'His imagery is particularly striking, and forges a character of its own. Evans has the ability to weave very physical detail in among more abstract concepts; the effect is oddly real and surreal.'

**John Foulcher**, *Canberra Times*

'Poetry of a very high quality indeed, understated in its treatment, and its impact is the stronger in consequence.'

*Social Alternatives*

'Steve Evans is developing as a major poet. His craftsmanship is impressive, language honed to be the instrument of sharp intellect, wit, and observation.'

**Hugh Oakes**, *Mattoid*

*Graham Rowlands*

# Selected Poems

Over the last twenty years, Graham Rowlands has gained a reputation as a one-man poetry industry. His six published collections of poetry contain only a fraction of his prodigious output. There have been weeks when the pages of literally any newspaper or journal in the country – from the *Australian* to the *Egglayers' Gazette* – could be opened and a Rowlands poem discovered.

'He has the ability to effectively manipulate the spoken word as few Australian poets do.'

**John Foulcher**, *Canberra Times*

'Rowlands has the irritating habit of producing fabulous poetry at a speed most court reporters would envy.'

**Howard Firkin**, *Verso*

'At the centre of a world of which he is both critical and despairing is a highly perceptive intellect.'

**Carol Treloar**, *Advertiser*

'He is a people's poet, a poet of public performances and pen-portraits on subjects as diverse as Galileo, T.S. Eliot, James McAuley and Jean Paul Sartre.'

**Warrick Wynne**, *Australian Book Review*

'A sharp eye, an original mind, a lucid style and ear for cadences and, above all, a compassionate understanding of human limitations.'

**Carmel Gaffney**, *Northern Perspective*

*Jeri Kroll*

# Monster Love
*and*
# House Arrest

'Kroll's poems ring with wit, honesty and straight talking. She convinces in exactly the right manner.'

**Philip Salom**, *West Australian*

'Kroll's verse is freely handled, her language precise in metaphor, but easy in movement – an ease not to be achieved without considerable art.'

**Barbara Giles**, *Australian Book Review*

'These are poems full of a fresh verve. Here the universal is made personal and the personal made universal and that, truly, is how literature at its best mirrors and deepens our lives for us.'

**Kate Llewellyn**